The Book Of John

Steps to a Happier Life

by

JOHN RICHARD MARSH

Copyright

Copyright © 2018
by John Richard Marsh (O'Brien).

All rights reserved. No part of this publication may be
reproduced, distributed, or transmitted in any form or by any
means, including photocopying, recording, or other electronic or
mechanical methods, without the prior written permission of the
publisher.

This is a work of fiction. Names, characters, places, and incidents
either are the products of the author's imagination or are used
fictitiously. Any resemblance to actual persons, living or dead,
businesses, companies, events, or locales is entirely coincidental.

Printed in the United States of America

First Printing, 2018
IngramSparks
ISBN-13: 978-1-7322904-0-2
ISBN-10: 1-7322904-0-7

Publisher: *JRM Productions*
John Richard Marsh Productions
1200 Paseo Camarillo, Suite 275A
Camarillo, CA 93010
http://www.jrm-production.com/
Facebook: **https://www.facebook.com/john.obrien.3726**
Cover & Interior Design: Carol Malone
Editors: Claudia Jane O'Brien, Judith Mathison, and Carol Malone
1. Self-help 2. Happiness 3. Motivational and Inspirational 4.
Personal Growth 5. Success 6. Spirituality

DEDICATION

To my wife: Claudia (Jane) O'Brien, A.K.A. Sunshine.
She has inspired me to enjoy life
and all I have been blessed with.

To my family who have loved me in spite of the challenges
I put them through.

To my friends who accept me for who I am.

Thank you for the opportunity to live a happier life.

ACKNOWLEDGMENTS

To Rod Brown, without whom I would not have been able to follow my dream of writing books.

To Carol Malone, who takes my story ideas and turns them into manuscripts.

Table of Contents

Steps to a Happier Life 1
Good Health– Physical and Mental... 2
Understanding Yourself... 4
Becoming the BEST You 6
Achieving Real and Lasting Happiness... 8
(Yes, it is possible!)... 8
Financial Security 10
The Value of Education 14
The Expense of Living 16
Quality, Morals, and Values in Life 18
Achieving Success in Life 20
About The Author and Storyteller.. 23
Upcoming Book Releases 24
With gratitude to my readers... 26

Steps to a Happier Life

The following

information reflects

the knowledge and wisdom

I've gained over my lifetime.

I desire to share them with you,

my friends, in the hopes you'll find

something you could identify with or

use to make your life happier and your

attitude positive, and fill your life with love.

Watch that first step,

John Richard Marsh

Good Health– Physical and Mental

- Good mental health is what helps to keep everything working for you. If you look for *things* to make you happy, you'll never be happy. Happy is a choice.

- If there is a different life you want to live, explore ways to make the hard changes.

- Physical health requires effort. To keep all your body parts working, do exercises of some kind every day. It will add up to better mental and physical health.

- What you do to your body every day will result in good or bad health. It's your choice.

- Nutritional food is the fuel the body needs to keep working and help you to feel your best.

- Like a paycheck, good health is earned one minute, hour, day, month, and year at a time.

- Good, healthy choices can help you determine what kind of a day you're going to have.

- Good health is a place you choose to go, not a place you are sent.

- Today's good health is a result of yesterday's decisions, so take advantage of the opportunities when they present themselves.

- *Today is the first day of the rest of your life.* If you want better health, change your mindset, and move forward.

Not one

of us is perfect.

No one is constantly in

good health all the time. We

all can do better at working toward

our healthy goals. We can be gentle and

remind ourselves to keep trying to do our

best each day of our lives – do it consistently.

Understanding Yourself

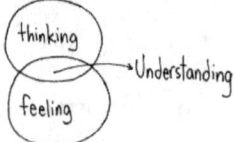

- You are the most important person in your life. Fill your bucket first, then help others.

- You can learn to love yourself, even knowing the real you.

- Remember all the things you are grateful for in your life, even during difficult times.

- Do your best every day, using all the help you can get. Perfection is not a place we can arrive at by ourselves. It's what we strive for.

- Don't sell yourself short. Feeling good is the emotion we achieve as we move beyond the struggles of our past.

- You can serve others and worry less about your own difficulties. Be a real blessing to yourself and others.

- You are a gift to the world. Share your experiences – good and bad – teach from your heart.

- You can influence a thousand people in a life time; help them grow into the best person possible.

- You can help your family achieve their goals in life.

- You're the only person who can plan for and achieve your own goals.

The

rewards

are great. Bad

experiences are for

your good. Good and bad

experiences make life worth the

pain. Who you become develops

over a lifetime of effort and hard work.

Becoming the BEST You

- What you want to become begins with your good decisions. To achieve this, you must believe choosing wisely will make your life better.

- Changing sometimes involves imitating the best qualities in other people who have achieved your ideal. Mirror them, but don't envy them.

- People make mistakes. Learn from them and don't make the same mistakes yourself.

- If your life has major problems, write them down in order of significance. They'll be more manageable. Work on one at a time.

- Be happy for what you are now and what you will become later. Compare you to you.

- Finding someone to make you happy is nearly impossible. Decide to be happy and good folks will find you.

- Becoming what you want to be is a life-long journey. Start today.

- When you become who you want to be, you'll notice the good things around you.

- Enjoy the experience of learning about yourself and then help others discover themselves.

- What you want to become will be hard work, but you're worth it.

If you are

not who you

want to be yet,

join the rest of us.

Setting goals, writing

them down, will help you

clarify your path. Perseverance

can push you forward to achieve

your goals. Keep at it. Developing a

positive attitude is the most important

trait you can cultivate to keep moving ahead.

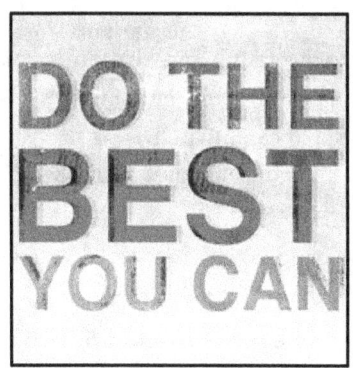

Achieving Real and Lasting Happiness
(Yes, it is possible!)

- Happiness comes as you work toward a goal with real desire. Take action today.

- Happiness is not a destination but a journey of discovery. You choose it over other emotions. No one can *make* you happy.

- Happiness is achieved by hanging out with positive people, or doing things which enhance positive experiences. It's contagious – pass it on.

- If you are not happy, choose a happy place in your head to visit until you can restore your happy.

- Happiness can be achieved by doing service for others; it makes you feel good to lift another.

- Allowing others to serve you will make them happy and you too.

- People were not put here to be miserable. You are here to experience the opportunities and joys of life.

- If you need help, get help. We often have times when we can't fix the difficulties in our lives. Don't be discouraged or ashamed – be proactive.

- Bad things happen to everyone. How you handle adversity makes all the difference.

- Happiness is the state of mind when you like yourself today, then work to do even better tomorrow.

Money or possessions don't equal real happiness. Choosing to be happy helps you to feel good about your life. Happiness can be the emotion within your heart that helps you smile. Some days you have to grit your teeth, smile, and *fake it till you make it*.

Financial Security

- Needs Vs. Wants. Fulfilled needs help us feel secure. Our wants can overwhelm us and ruin us financially.
- Banks aren't your friend. They're in business to make money. Beware of the hidden charges and fees. You don't want to give away your hard-earned money.
- Credit cards are not good. They mortgage your future income. Avoid debt like the plague.
- Buy only what you need. Everything else is stuff you have to maintain and store. Young people expect to have what it took their parents years to acquire. Be patient.
- Buy the very best you can afford and you will be content. Buy the cheapest, and you will never be satisfied.
- How people become wealthy is simple. They don't buy junk that has no value.
- There are no special gifts in heaven for having the most junk in your garage.
- *You'll never have enough stuff you don't need.*
- You can be rich when what you need is purchased with cash, and what you want, you save up for ... and purchase in cash.
- A rich man's budget works 100% of the time: If you earn $1.00 – give $.10 away, save $.10, live on $.80. The dime you give away will come back to you in unnumbered blessings when you need them.

Credit Cards:

a necessary evil?

Mistakes – don't worry,

just keep moving forward.

Financial security, trust me,

you won't get there immediately.

If a problem can be fixed with money,

it is not really a problem. If you buy a

hamburger for $5.00 on a credit card

and don't pay it off at the month's end,

you will eventually pay $25.00 in interest.

Your Value and Your Worth

- I believe that every soul counts and you are no different. We are here to learn, experience, grow, and become the best we can become.

- My grandmother says good quality never loses value. Reach for the potential hiding within you.

- Hardships are a big part of life and the experience we gain is invaluable. You have to experience the bitter to enjoy the sweet.

- You count because you are unique. So enjoy the blessings of who you are and can become.

- Opinions from others are observations from their experiences and perspective, not necessarily truth.

- Rich or poor is not the sum total of your value. What you believe about yourself is of the greatest worth. Remembering who you are and what type of person you have the potential to become is also important.

- The most significant gift you have to give is you. You are not a mistake. You have challenges like everyone else. If you compare yourself to others you will always come up short and be disappointed.

- You count because our maker does not make mistakes and you are *not* a mistake.

- You have worth for the benefit of serving and assisting others with the problems in their lives.

- Don't let your problems determine who you are, let them help you in living out your life.

You can

be the lamb

or the wolf. You

become one of those

by whichever you feed.

The world will never give

us what we want to be happy.

Your self-esteem and worth count,

and you can make life a nice place for you.

The Value of Education

- Education comes from what we learn each day. We use that knowledge to aid us throughout our whole life. Do not waste the opportunity to gain wisdom.
- Not everyone attends a university for formal education. Still, everyone needs to get an education of some kind – the kind that fits you.
- It is not the expense of your education, but the value of what you learn that counts.
- Schooling is where you start the process of learning. Education is when you value what you have learned.
- If you believe in yourself, you'll know if you need to continue the education that works for you and your life choices. Be proactive.
- The lack of education will be the most expensive lesson you will ever learn.
- A formal education helps. However, is not the sign of success or failure, but of opportunity.
- Pursue the education that makes you valuable in earning a living.
- People who are fortunate enough to acquire a great education, don't always have good lives. It's how you use your education that matters.
- If you are happy with who you are, experiences and formal education will help you enjoy a good life.

Don't Quit

learning after

you leave school.

Education is not what

helps you become wealthy.

Education gives you a head

start to earning a good living.

Many folks graduate from the

University of Hard Knocks and

succeed. Many people take years to

get their college degrees. Do not despair.

The Expense of Living

- Make a budget of what you need to live comfortably; then adhere to your budget. Save when you can.
- Too much stuff clutters your mind, house, and life; don't let stuff make you poor. Let life make you rich.
- If you can't afford it and buy it anyway, you will always be unhappy with what you have.
- You will never own enough stuff to make you happy.
- Possessions won't bring you happiness. Being grateful for your life and your blessing will bring happiness.
- Garage stuffers are things you won't get rid of, but no longer fit in your house. When you can't park two cars in a two-car garage, you have too much stuff.
- It is less expensive to enjoy what you have and spend your time with those you love.
- Nothing you possess will ever impress those who have more than you, and will cause envy for those who have less.
- Real living is not measured by who has the most stuff.
- Expensive living is when you have it all and you're still not satisfied or happy.

Stuff never
made anyone happy.
90% of what people own is
of no real value. People spend the
majority of their lives acquiring too
much stuff. Stuff is bad when it makes
you want more than what you already have.

Quality, Morals, and Values in Life

- Good values and good morals never go out of style.

- Experience and education give you a quality of life that cannot be taken away.

- Special value is found in the daily things that happen to you along life's journey. Appreciate them.

- High morals will make your pursuit of happiness worth the effort and you a more desirable person.

- Values and morals give us the strength to get through the really tough parts of life.

- Cultivate a good moral character and you will be blessed every day. Fill your bucket with good deeds and you will reap the benefit.

- By helping to serve others, you add value to their lives and will enjoy your own. Besides, it just makes you feel good.

- Our families observe our moral behavior and hopefully, they'll mirror us.

- Our values help us understand what is important and what is of no worth.

- Morals and values raise the quality of life and become the principles on which we base our behavior.

What we

value helps us

to stand out, both

good and bad. Quality,

values, and good morals

raise our standard of living.

Special values comes from learning

how important our lives are. A quality

life, good morals, and abiding values help us

enjoy our lives to the fullest, and share with others

Achieving Success in Life

- Being successful is 90% failure and 10% success. Don't count the failures.

- Success is built on doing something positive every day and for the entire length of your lifetime.

- Success is earned by cultivating a positive attitude toward what you do and how you do it, or making a change to something better.

- Money is a reward you receive on your way to success.

- Successful people have good habits they work on each day.

- Success is only achieved by working on what you want to accomplish.

- Success is a measurement of what you have achieved. But loving others is also success.

- You can be happy and successful if you enjoy your own achievements, then work to do even better.

- Becoming successful is not always measured by what others think of you. They will always move the yardstick.

- You will be successful every day by waking up and doing the very best you can in spite of what life throws your way.

Success

is believing in

yourself. Success is

bettering yourself and

those around you. Become

the very best person you can be

and choose to be happy. Don't envy

others. Their lives might look perfect,

but it's not always true.

> Yes we can
>
> Think positive
>
> Trust in yourself
>
> Never stop learning
>
> All things are possible
>
> *Love to you all,*
> *John*

ABOUT THE AUTHOR AND STORYTELLER
John Richard Marsh (O'Brien)

I love to tell stories and have been a storyteller all my life. I want to share them with my friends and fans. My background is not typical for an author. I have had careers in manufacturing, selling, commercial construction, mortgage brokering, and now as an author.

I have enjoyed being married to my wife for thirty-seven years and she still likes me. We have four children, four grand-children, and two great-grand-children. What a blessed life I have been given.

My production company and I, JRM Productions, share compelling stories so our readers will find more enjoyment in their lives, and maybe even a change of heart.

I am a member of the Ventura County Writers Club and enjoy working with other authors as we "Encourage the Craft" of writing.

I am the author of three books: *The Book of John, The Secret of Sunrise Mountain,* and *Sunrise Ranch.* The last two are historical epics following the lives of one family through the generations as they traverse the American Continent settling in Placer County, California, with all the tragedies and hardships that accompany tough ranch life.

You can find me at: http://jrm-productions.com/

Facebook: https://www.facebook.com/john.obrien.3726

John Richard Marsh
Author

UPCOMING BOOK RELEASES

Sunrise Ranch – A Search for Home
Book 1: Sunrise Mountain Series

In the tradition of C.J. Box and his Joe Pickett classic western novels, and Craig Johnson's Longmire mysteries comes a new epic series.

1906 - Elmer Johnson's dream is to chug across America aboard the smoke-belching locomotives of the G.N.R.R. And though Elmer and his best friend have spectacular adventures, death stalks them at every turn.

Elmer finds his passion in the striking blue eyes of a bold and sassy Norwegian girl, Olina, and the raw, untamed beauty of ranch land of Placer County, California. But ranch life is not idyllic for Elmer and Olina when someone wants their ranch and will stop at nothing to possess it ... and Olina.

Surviving cattle rustlers, drought, the Depression, and the World Wars, were nothing compared to the bitter hatred of someone filled with prejudice who's threatening to kill them.

Coming: Fall of 2018

Murder on Sunrise Ranch
Book 2: Sunrise Mountain Series

In the tradition of C.J. Box and his Joe Pickett classic western novels, and Craig Johnson's Longmire mysteries comes a new epic series.

A riveting epic western historical about a panicked rancher, Bert Johnson's quest to investigate his murder charge.

Coming: spring 2019

The Secret of Sunrise Mountain
Book 3: Sunrise Mountain Series

In the tradition of C.J. Box and his Joe Pickett classic western novels, and Craig Johnson's Longmire mysteries comes a new epic series.

1998 – someone or something is stampeding widower rancher Joe Mack's cattle threatening his livelihood and killing precious heifers and calves.

The local sheriff won't help. He relishes punishing Joe for "ruining" his life, so Joe is forced to take matters into his own hands.

When his friends are beaten up and shot, his new gal nearly killed, Joe finds himself in the middle of a war with mercenaries facing the deadly possibility of losing everyone and everything he holds dear.

Coming: spring of 2018

Saving Sunrise Ranch
Book 4: Sunrise Mountain Series

In the tradition of C.J. Box and his Joe Pickett classic western novels, and Craig Johnson's Longmire mysteries comes a new epic series.

An unforgettable sage about a discouraged rancher's son, Jake Mack, and his hesitant girlfriend, Olivia Meyers's struggle to confront their desire and save the ranch from failure.

Coming: fall of 2019

With gratitude to my readers,

Thank you for reading my little book. I am so pleased you took a chance and read the short pages and the challenges contained within. I hope something from my *Steps to a Happier Life* will touch your heart.

If you found an aspect within the pages of my little book, *Steps to a Happier Life*, to help change your life, and you feel it deserves a 4- or 5-Star rating, please leave a review on Amazon where my books are listed. Reviews for an author are like standing ovations to an onstage performer – only sweeter because they last longer.

If you would like to comment about the book, please visit my website: http://jrm-productions.com/ and leave your thoughts, concerns, or celebrations. Please sign up for my newsletter or follow my blog of life-changing and humorous posts. Any of my friends can comment on my blog, and you are my friends.

I'm always eager to hear if something I said makes a difference in someone's life. Please feel free to contact me at jrmproductionsco@gmail.com.

www.ingramcontent.com/pod-product-compliance
Lightning Source LLC
Chambersburg PA
CBHW052046070526
44584CB00018B/2627